CILLIAN MURPHY

Biography of a Great Actor

Info Edge

Info Edge Publications

CONTENTS

CHAPTER 1: INTRODUCTION

The allure of Cillian Murphy's enigmatic persona and his extraordinary journey through the world of acting have captivated audiences and critics alike. This biography aims to delve into the life and career of the enigmatic Irish actor, known for his chameleon-like ability to embody a diverse range of characters on screen and stage. From his humble beginnings in County Cork, Ireland, to his international acclaim as one of the most talented actors of his generation, Cillian Murphy's story is a testament to his dedication, talent, and pursuit of artistic excellence.

Early Life and Background

Cillian Murphy was born on May 25, 1976, in Douglas, a suburb of Cork, Ireland. He grew up in a close-knit family, with his parents and two siblings. From a young age, he displayed an innate curiosity and a vivid imagination, traits that would later serve him well in his acting career. While he initially harbored dreams of becoming a musician, fate had other plans in store for him.

Discovering the World of Acting

As a teenager, Cillian Murphy discovered a passion for the performing arts. He became involved in school plays and local theatre productions, where he honed his acting skills and began to realize the transformative power of the craft. His early experiences on stage fuelled a desire to pursue acting professionally, but it was not a decision made lightly. The path of an actor is often uncertain and challenging, yet Cillian's determination to follow his dreams remained unwavering.

Education and Training

To prepare for a career in acting, Cillian Murphy sought formal training. He attended the Presentation Brothers College in Cork and later enrolled in the Drama and Theatre Studies program at the University College Cork. During this time, he immersed himself in the world of drama, studying the works of influential playwrights and participating in various productions. His dedication and commitment to his craft were evident, and it was during his university years that he began to see acting not just as a hobby, but as his true calling.

Breaking into the Industry

After completing his education, Cillian Murphy faced the daunting challenge of breaking into the highly competitive world of acting. Like many aspiring actors, he encountered numerous rejections and setbacks. However, his perseverance paid off when he landed his first professional role in a stage production of "Disco Pigs" in 1996. The play garnered critical acclaim, and Cillian's raw talent and magnetic stage presence quickly caught the attention of theatre critics and industry insiders.

Rising Star: Breakthrough Performances

With his initial success on the stage, Cillian Murphy set his sights on conquering the world of film. In 2002, he received a career-defining opportunity when he was cast as Jim, the lead role in Danny Boyle's post-apocalyptic horror film, "28 Days Later." The film became a commercial and critical success, introducing Cillian to a global audience and establishing him as a rising star in the film industry.

Exploring Iconic Roles

Following the success of "28 Days Later," Cillian Murphy continued to take on challenging and diverse roles, proving his versatility as an actor. In 2005, he portrayed the menacing and enigmatic Scarecrow in Christopher Nolan's "Batman Begins," a role he would reprise in the film's sequels. His ability to portray complex and multifaceted characters earned him accolades and further cemented his reputation as a formidable talent in Hollywood.

Embracing the Stage

While finding success in the world of film, Cillian Murphy never strayed far from his first love – the theatre. He returned to the stage in between film projects, starring in productions like "The Shape of Things," "The Seagull," and "Misterman." His passion for live performances remained unwavering, and critics continued to praise his commitment to each role he undertook.

The Art of Transformation

One of the most remarkable aspects of Cillian Murphy's acting prowess is his ability to undergo radical physical and emotional transformations for his roles. Whether it is losing weight, altering his appearance, or mastering different accents, he fully immerses himself in each character, leaving audiences astounded by his dedication and authenticity.

Collaborations and Relationships

Throughout his career, Cillian Murphy has had the privilege of working with acclaimed directors and talented co-stars. His collaborations with visionary filmmakers like Christopher Nolan and Ken Loach have resulted in some of his most memorable performances. Additionally, his chemistry with fellow actors has elevated the impact of his roles and contributed to the success of the projects in which he's been involved.

Balancing Fame and Privacy

Despite achieving fame and recognition, Cillian Murphy has managed to maintain a remarkably private personal life. He values his privacy and strives to keep his family and personal relationships out of the spotlight, a rarity in today's celebrity-driven culture. This chapter explores his approach to fame and how he navigates the fine line between public and private life.

In the subsequent chapters, we will delve deeper into Cillian Murphy's personal life, career milestones, challenges, and triumphs, exploring the legacy he is building and the mark he leaves on the world of acting. From his humble beginnings in Ireland to his status as an internationally acclaimed actor, Cillian's journey is one of dedication, passion, and an unwavering commitment to his craft. So, join us as we unravel the layers of this enigmatic artist and gain insight into the captivating world of Cillian Murphy.

CHAPTER 2: EARLY LIFE AND BACKGROUND

C illian Murphy's journey as a remarkable actor was shaped by his formative years and the experiences that laid the foundation for his extraordinary career. Born on May 25, 1976, in Douglas, a suburb of Cork, Ireland, Cillian was raised in a close-knit family that instilled in him the values of hard work, creativity, and a love for the arts.

Childhood in County Cork

Growing up in County Cork, Ireland's largest county known for its lush landscapes and rich cultural heritage, Cillian experienced a childhood that would leave an indelible mark on his life. His parents, Brendan, and Maureen Murphy, were both educators who nurtured a supportive and intellectually stimulating environment at home. Cillian's upbringing encouraged curiosity and exploration, allowing him to develop a keen interest in literature, music, and the performing arts from a young age.

A Creative Spark

From the early years of his life, it was evident that Cillian possessed a creative spark. He would often lose himself in books, immersing himself in stories that transported him to far-off places and introduced him to a multitude of characters. This love for storytelling would become a fundamental aspect of his future career, as the essence of acting lies in bringing characters and narratives to life on stage and screen.

The Influence of Music

As a child, Cillian Murphy initially aspired to become a musician. His fascination with music led him to explore various instruments, and he eventually learned to play the guitar and sing. Music became an outlet for his emotions and artistic expression, and it provided him with a sense of solace during both joyful and challenging times.

Academic Pursuits and the Seeds of Theatre

In addition to his creative pursuits, Cillian excelled academically. He attended the Presentation Brothers College in Cork, where he demonstrated a natural aptitude for academics. While he dedicated himself to his studies, he never lost sight of his love for the arts.

It was during his time at school that Cillian's interest in theatre began to take root. He participated in school plays and local theatre productions, seizing every opportunity to showcase his acting abilities. These early experiences on the stage ignited a passion within him and set him on a course that would ultimately define his life's purpose.

The Decision to Pursue Acting

As Cillian Murphy approached the crossroads of choosing a career path, he faced the common dilemma that many aspiring artists encounter. While he had a natural talent for academics, a part of him yearned for a life in the arts, where he could explore the depths of human emotions and connect with audiences through the power of storytelling.

After much soul-searching and contemplation,

Cillian made the pivotal decision to pursue acting professionally. It was a bold choice, one that carried inherent risks and uncertainties, but he was determined to follow his heart and fulfill his dreams.

Nurturing the Craft

With a newfound sense of purpose, Cillian Murphy sought to refine his acting skills and immerse himself in the world of drama. He recognized the importance of formal training and decided to enroll in the Drama and Theatre Studies program at the University College Cork.

During his time at the university, Cillian's dedication to his craft became evident to his professors and peers. He approached his studies with a relentless commitment to learning and growing as an actor. By exploring various theatrical styles and delving into the works of influential playwrights, he expanded his artistic horizons and gained a deeper appreciation for the intricacies of the performing arts.

The Influence of Cork's Artistic Community

Cork's vibrant artistic community played a significant role in shaping Cillian Murphy's early years as an actor. The city's thriving theatre scene provided him with opportunities to participate in local productions and collaborate with seasoned actors and directors. These experiences allowed him to gain valuable insights into the world of professional theatre and solidify his aspirations to make a career out of acting.

Family Support and Encouragement

Throughout his journey, Cillian Murphy was fortunate to have unwavering support from his family. His parents played an instrumental role in nurturing his dreams and encouraging him to pursue his passion for acting. Their belief in his talent and potential gave him the confidence to forge ahead despite the challenges that lay ahead.

In conclusion, Cillian Murphy's early life and background laid the groundwork for the exceptional actor he would become. Growing up in County Cork, Ireland, surrounded by a loving family and a vibrant artistic community, Cillian's creative instincts were nurtured from a young age. His passion for storytelling, kindled by a love for literature and music, eventually led him to the world of acting. With the decision to pursue a career in theatre and film, Cillian embarked on a path that would test his determination, resilience, and commitment to his art. The subsequent chapters will explore how these formative years and influences shaped the trajectory of his career, propelling him toward becoming one of the most celebrated actors of his generation.

CHAPTER 3: THE PATH TO ACTING

C illian Murphy's journey to becoming a renowned actor was marked by dedication, perseverance, and a relentless pursuit of his passion for the performing arts. Chapter 3 delves into the crucial phase of his life when he actively pursued acting as a career, seeking formal training and embracing opportunities that would shape him into the versatile and enigmatic actor he is known as today.

A Defining Choice

Upon graduating from the Drama and Theatre Studies program at the University College Cork, Cillian Murphy faced a pivotal crossroads in his life. Armed with his newfound knowledge and honed acting skills, he had to decide how to channel his passion for the arts into a fulfilling career. This defining choice required courage, as the path of an actor is often fraught with uncertainty and challenges.

With unwavering determination and a belief in his abilities, Cillian resolved to take the plunge into the world of professional acting. He knew that success in the field would require hard work, tenacity, and a willingness to embrace every opportunity, no matter how small or challenging.

Theatre: A Training Ground

In the early stages of his acting career, Cillian Murphy recognized the importance of gaining experience on stage. He understood that the theatre would serve as an invaluable training ground, providing him with the opportunity to refine his craft and develop his unique style of performance.

He began auditioning for various theatrical productions, both in Cork and beyond, gradually building a reputation as a committed and talented actor. His early roles may have been modest in scale, but they allowed him to grow as an artist, exploring a diverse range of characters and narratives that contributed to his artistic growth.

The Impact of "Disco Pigs"

A turning point in Cillian Murphy's theatrical journey came in 1996 when he was cast in the role of Pig in the play "Disco Pigs" by Irish playwright Enda Walsh. The play was an intense and emotionally charged exploration of a close friendship between two teenagers who share a deep bond but are gradually torn apart by their disparate aspirations.

Cillian's portrayal of the complex and volatile character of Pig garnered critical acclaim and put him firmly on the map as a rising star in Irish theatre. The rawness and vulnerability he brought to the role demonstrated a level of talent that caught the attention of theatre critics and directors, earning him accolades and recognition within the theatrical community.

Expanding Horizons: The Move to London

Fuelled by the success of "Disco Pigs," Cillian Murphy sought to further expand his horizons and challenge himself as an actor. He made the significant decision to move to London, a city renowned for its thriving performing arts scene and a plethora of opportunities for emerging actors.

London offered Cillian exposure to a diverse array of theatre productions, ranging from classic plays to avant-garde performances. He embraced the city's vibrant cultural landscape, immersing himself in the richness of its theatre tradition, and sought auditions that would allow him to continue honing his craft.

From Theatre to Television

In addition to his stage work, Cillian Murphy ventured into the realm of television, recognizing it as another avenue for growth and exposure. He secured roles in a variety of television series, demonstrating his versatility in adapting to the demands of the screen.

One notable early television role came in the form of a BBC production titled "The Way We Live Now" (2001), where he portrayed the character of Paul Montague, a young man entangled in a romantic and financial drama. This performance showcased Cillian's ability to convey emotional depth and complexity, laying the groundwork for his future successes on the screen.

Cillian Murphy's Artistic Signature

Throughout this phase of his career, Cillian Murphy began to develop his artistic signature – a unique blend of intensity, vulnerability, and a subtle yet magnetic screen presence. His dedication to each role, his meticulous approach to character development, and his willingness to take risks set him apart as an actor committed to the art of storytelling.

His choices in roles demonstrated a penchant for complex and morally ambiguous characters, further fuelling the intrigue surrounding his enigmatic persona. Cillian was drawn to narratives that challenged both the audience and himself, seeking projects that explored the intricacies of the human condition and offered opportunities for personal growth and artistic exploration.

The Fruit of Perseverance: Recognition and Acclaim

As Cillian Murphy continued to sharpen his skills and immerse himself in diverse acting opportunities, his talent did not go unnoticed. The theatre and television communities began to take note of the young Irish actor's extraordinary potential, and he earned nominations and awards for his outstanding performances.

The Turning Point: "28 Days Later"

In 2002, Cillian Murphy's trajectory as an actor took a momentous turn when he was cast in the lead role of Jim in the post-apocalyptic horror film "28 Days Later," directed by Danny Boyle. This film would prove to be a milestone in Cillian's career, propelling him to international acclaim and introducing him to a broader global audience.

His portrayal of Jim, a survivor in a world ravaged by a deadly virus, showcased the full range of his acting abilities, from vulnerability to courage and determination. "28 Days Later" became a commercial success and garnered widespread critical praise, solidifying Cillian's position as a rising star in the film industry.

Conclusion

Chapter 3 illuminates the pivotal phase of Cillian Murphy's journey into the world of acting. From his decision to pursue a career in theatre and his experiences on the stage to his move to London and eventual foray into television and film, Cillian's unwavering dedication to his craft shone through.

With each role and performance, Cillian Murphy's

acting prowess evolved, and he continued to develop his unique artistic signature. The success of "Disco Pigs" and the breakthrough role in "28 Days Later" opened doors for him, leading him toward a path of international acclaim and acclaim.

In the subsequent chapters, we will delve further into Cillian's remarkable career, exploring his rising status in Hollywood, his memorable collaborations with acclaimed directors and co-stars, and the challenges he faced in balancing fame with a desire for privacy. Join us as we uncover the layers of this enigmatic artist and the legacy he continues to build in the world of acting.

CHAPTER 4:
BREAKING INTO
THE INDUSTRY

After the success of "28 Days Later," Cillian Murphy found himself on the cusp of a burgeoning acting career. Chapter 4 explores the transformative period when Cillian transitioned from a talented actor to an internationally recognized star, breaking into the film industry and making his mark on the global stage.

Gaining Traction in Hollywood

Following the critical acclaim, he received for his role in "28 Days Later," Cillian Murphy's talent did not go unnoticed in Hollywood. Directors and casting agents were intrigued by his unique blend of intensity, vulnerability, and charisma. Offers for a variety of roles started to come his way, but Cillian remained selective, opting for projects that aligned with his artistic sensibilities.

In 2003, he starred alongside Naomie Harris in "28 Weeks Later," the sequel to the hit horror film. The movie further solidified his standing in the genre and showcased his ability to carry a film as a leading actor.

Collaborating with Christopher Nolan

A defining moment in Cillian Murphy's career came when he was cast as the villainous Dr. Jonathan Crane, aka Scarecrow, in Christopher Nolan's "Batman Begins" (2005). Nolan's reimagining of the iconic superhero breathed new life into the Batman franchise, and Cillian's portrayal of the menacing Scarecrow garnered widespread praise.

Working with Christopher Nolan marked the beginning of a fruitful collaboration that would continue to define Cillian's Hollywood journey. Nolan was impressed by Cillian's ability to bring depth and complexity to his characters, and their partnership would extend to future projects, cementing Cillian's position as a sought-after actor in major Hollywood productions.

"Red Eye" and Hollywood Thrillers

In 2005, Cillian Murphy further showcased his versatility by taking on a different genre. He starred opposite Rachel McAdams in the thriller "Red Eye," directed by Wes Craven. In this gripping film, he portrayed a charming yet sinister character who terrorizes McAdams' character during a flight. The film's success demonstrated Cillian's ability to captivate audiences in diverse roles, solidifying his reputation as a dynamic actor capable of portraying a wide range of characters.

"Sunshine" and Continuing Collaborations

Continuing his collaboration with Christopher Nolan, Cillian Murphy appeared in "The Dark Knight" (2008), the second installment in Nolan's Batman trilogy, reprising his role as Scarecrow. This marked his third collaboration with Nolan, showcasing the trust and respect the director had for Cillian's talent.

Additionally, Cillian reunited with director Danny Boyle in "Sunshine" (2007), a sci-fi thriller set in the future where a team of astronauts embarks on a mission to reignite the dying sun. His portrayal of physicist Robert Capa once again demonstrated his ability to anchor a film with emotional depth and complexity, reaffirming his standing as a reliable and compelling leading actor.

Embracing Independent Cinema

While gaining prominence in Hollywood, Cillian Murphy remained committed to independent cinema and projects that explored unique and thought-provoking narratives. His dedication to the art of storytelling led him to collaborate with visionary directors in independent productions that challenged the conventions of mainstream cinema.

In 2005, Cillian starred in "Breakfast on Pluto," directed by Neil Jordan, in which he played a transgender woman navigating life in 1970s Ireland and London. The film showcased Cillian's willingness to take on unconventional and daring roles that explored complex themes with sensitivity and authenticity.

Critical Acclaim: "The Wind That Shakes the Barley"

Cillian Murphy's artistic choices and commitment to authenticity were further validated when he starred in Ken Loach's "The Wind That Shakes the Barley" (2006). This historical drama explored the Irish War of Independence and Civil War, a subject matter deeply rooted in Irish history and culture. Cillian portrayed Damien O'Donovan, a young medical graduate who becomes embroiled in the fight for independence.

His nuanced performance earned him widespread critical acclaim and a Silver Bear for Best Actor at the Berlin International Film Festival. "The Wind That Shakes the Barley" showcased Cillian's ability to embody the emotional complexity of a character and highlighted his willingness to engage with projects that held cultural significance.

"Inception" and International Stardom

One of the defining moments in Cillian Murphy's career came with his role as Robert Fischer in Christopher Nolan's mind-bending sci-fi thriller "Inception" (2010). The film brought together a star-studded cast and explored complex themes of dreams and reality.

Cillian's portrayal of Fischer, a target of the film's protagonist, showcased his versatility as an actor, seamlessly shifting between vulnerability and determination. "Inception" became a worldwide blockbuster and catapulted Cillian into international stardom, solidifying his position as one of Hollywood's most compelling and versatile actors.

Maintaining Artistic Integrity

Despite the allure of fame and success, Cillian Murphy remained committed to maintaining his artistic integrity. He continued to seek projects that challenged him creatively and allowed him to explore the depths of human emotion and psyche. Whether in Hollywood blockbusters or independent productions, he consistently delivered authentic and captivating performances.

Conclusion

Chapter 4 explores the transformative phase of Cillian Murphy's career, as he broke into the film industry and made his mark as an internationally acclaimed actor. His collaborations with visionary directors like Christopher Nolan and Danny Boyle, along with his commitment to diverse and challenging roles, solidified his reputation as a formidable talent in Hollywood and beyond.

Cillian's artistic choices and dedication to his craft set him apart as an actor who embraced growth opportunities and sought projects that resonated with him on a deeper level. As he continued to evolve as an actor, the world began to recognize the enigmatic allure and raw talent that defined Cillian Murphy as one of the most captivating performers of his generation.

In the subsequent chapters, we will explore Cillian's collaborations, his personal and professional growth, and the impact of his unique artistic signature on the entertainment industry. Join us as we journey through the life and career of this enigmatic actor, unveiling the layers that make him a true icon in the world of acting.

CHAPTER 5: RISING STAR: BREAKTHROUGH PERFORMANCES

With a series of impressive roles and critically acclaimed performances under his belt, Cillian Murphy emerged as a rising star in the entertainment industry. Chapter 5 delves into the pivotal period of his career when he solidified his status as a talented and versatile actor through breakthrough roles that captivated audiences and critics alike.

"Peacock" - A Showcase of Versatility

In 2010, Cillian Murphy delivered a tour de force performance in the psychological thriller "Peacock."

The film showcased his remarkable versatility as he portrayed dual characters – John Skillpa, a shy and introverted bank clerk, and Emma, his vivacious alter ego. Cillian's ability to inhabit two contrasting personalities within the same character demonstrated his nuanced approach to storytelling and earned him praise for his exceptional acting range.

"The Perks of Being a Wallflower" - Emotional Depth

Cillian Murphy's ability to convey emotional depth and vulnerability was once again on display in the coming-of-age drama "The Perks of Being a Wallflower" (2012). In a supporting role as Bill, a compassionate and understanding high school teacher, he left a lasting impact on the audience. His portrayal of Bill's struggles and resilience served as a testament to his skill in bringing depth and authenticity to even smaller roles.

"Broken" - Heartfelt and Poignant

In the British drama "Broken" (2012), Cillian Murphy delivered a heartfelt and poignant performance as Mike, a single father struggling to cope with the complexities of modern family life. The film's exploration of love, loss, and compassion allowed Cillian to showcase his ability to convey a range of emotions, further solidifying his reputation as a deeply affecting actor capable of evoking empathy from audiences.

"Peaky Blinders" - Tommy Shelby

Perhaps one of the most iconic roles of Cillian Murphy's career came in the form of Tommy Shelby, the enigmatic and cunning leader of a crime family in the acclaimed television series "Peaky Blinders." Premiering in 2013, the show was an instant hit, and Cillian's portrayal of Tommy Shelby earned widespread acclaim and a dedicated fan following.

As the central character of the series, Tommy Shelby required a complex and multi-layered performance, and Cillian delivered in spades. He masterfully portrayed the nuances of a man torn between his criminal endeavors and his desire for legitimacy, and his mesmerizing presence on screen became the cornerstone of the show's success.

"Transcendence" - Exploring Futuristic Themes

In the science-fiction thriller "Transcendence" (2014), Cillian Murphy starred alongside Johnny Depp and Rebecca Hall. His role as Agent Donald Buchanan, a skeptical government agent investigating the potential dangers of artificial intelligence, further demonstrated his ability to hold his own in major Hollywood productions.

The film's exploration of futuristic themes and ethical dilemmas allowed Cillian to engage with thought-provoking narratives while collaborating with a stellar cast and esteemed director Wally Pfister.

"A Quiet Place Part II" - A New Dimension

In 2021, Cillian Murphy joined the cast of the highly anticipated horror-thriller "A Quiet Place Part II." He played Emmett, a conflicted survivor trying to navigate a post-apocalyptic world plagued by deadly creatures that hunt by sound. Cillian's role as a weary and guarded ally added a new dimension to the film's tense and suspenseful narrative.

His presence in the film exemplified his ability to command attention on screen, regardless of the genre, and further solidified his status as a versatile actor who could excel in a wide range of roles.

Continued Theatre Pursuits

Despite his growing prominence in the film and television industry, Cillian Murphy continued to return to his first love – the theatre. He remained committed to the stage, taking on roles in various productions that allowed him to challenge himself artistically and connect with live audiences.

In 2017, he starred in the acclaimed play "Grief Is the Thing with Feathers," based on the novel by Max Porter. Cillian's portrayal of a bereaved husband and father was hailed as a tour de force, earning him widespread praise for his powerful and affecting performance.

The Influence of Christopher Nolan

Throughout this period of rising stardom, Cillian Murphy's collaboration with Christopher Nolan continued to play a significant role in his career. The director had become a staunch supporter of Cillian's talent, casting him in pivotal roles in his films.

In "Dunkirk" (2017), Nolan's war epic, Cillian portrayed a shell-shocked soldier, adding a touch of vulnerability to the harrowing wartime narrative. This collaboration further cemented Cillian's status as one of Nolan's most trusted and reliable collaborators.

Awards and Recognition

As Cillian Murphy's career soared, so did the recognition he received for his exceptional performances. His work in both film and television earned him nominations and awards from prestigious organizations, including the Irish Film and Television Awards and the London Critics' Circle Film Awards.

His remarkable range as an actor, coupled with his ability to embrace complex characters and emotionally charged narratives, garnered him praise from peers and critics alike, elevating him to the status of an actor's actor.

Conclusion

Chapter 5 explores the pivotal phase of Cillian Murphy's career as he ascended to stardom through breakthrough performances in film, television, and theatre. His ability to embody a wide array of characters and evoke genuine emotion resonated with audiences and critics alike, further solidifying his status as one of the most talented and versatile actors of his generation.

As he continued to challenge himself with diverse and complex roles, Cillian Murphy's enigmatic allure as an actor became increasingly evident. From his memorable portrayal of Tommy Shelby in "Peaky

Blinders" to his collaborations with visionary directors like Christopher Nolan, Cillian's career was marked by a relentless pursuit of artistic excellence.

In the following chapters, we will explore Cillian's collaborations, personal life, and his unique impact on the entertainment industry. Join us as we continue to uncover the layers of this enigmatic artist, revealing the legacy he is building and the mark he leaves on the world of acting.

CHAPTER 6:
EMBRACING
THE STAGE

Despite achieving international success on the big and small screens, Cillian Murphy remained deeply committed to his first love – the theatre. Chapter 6 delves into Cillian's enduring passion for the stage, his impressive achievements in theatre productions, and the profound impact of his live performances on both audiences and the broader artistic community.

The Theatre: A Homecoming

For Cillian Murphy, the theatre represented a homecoming of sorts – a return to his roots as an actor and a space where he could continually challenge and reinvent himself as an artist. Despite achieving fame in Hollywood, Cillian maintained a deep appreciation for the raw and intimate connection that only live theatre could provide.

The theatre offered him the opportunity to connect directly with audiences, sharing the immediacy of storytelling and experiencing the emotional responses in real-time. The stage also allowed him to collaborate with fellow actors and theatre professionals in a creative and collaborative environment that held a special place in his heart.

Returning to Ireland: "Ballyturk"

In 2014, Cillian Murphy returned to his native Ireland to star in the acclaimed play "Ballyturk." Written by Enda Walsh, with whom Cillian had previously collaborated on "Disco Pigs," the play delved into themes of identity, mortality, and the human condition. The production marked a significant reunion for the actor and playwright and garnered critical praise for Cillian's powerful and immersive performance.

"Ballyturk" showcased Cillian's deep understanding of the Irish theatrical tradition and his ability to breathe life into complex characters on stage. The play served as a testament to Cillian's enduring connection to his Irish roots and his continued commitment to the country's vibrant theatre scene.

Grief Is the Thing with Feathers

In 2018, Cillian Murphy's theatre prowess was once again on full display when he starred in the stage adaptation of Max Porter's novel "Grief Is the Thing with Feathers." The play, directed by Enda Walsh, explored themes of loss, grief, and healing in the aftermath of a tragic event.

Cillian's performance as a bereaved husband and father was hailed as a masterclass in emotional depth and vulnerability. His portrayal of the grieving character captivated audiences and earned him widespread acclaim from theatre critics. Once again, Cillian demonstrated his ability to connect with audiences on a profound and emotional level, showcasing the unique power of live theatre.

The Influence of Samuel Beckett

Cillian Murphy's dedication to the theatre extended beyond contemporary works. He also embraced the works of Samuel Beckett, one of Ireland's most renowned playwrights. Beckett's enigmatic and philosophical plays presented a unique set of challenges for actors, requiring a deep understanding of the text and a willingness to explore the complexities of the human condition.

In 2016, Cillian starred in a production of Beckett's "Endgame," alongside renowned actor Stephen Rea. The play, directed by Michael Colgan, received widespread acclaim and demonstrated Cillian's versatility as an actor, able to tackle works of classic theatre with a contemporary sensibility.

The National Theatre: "The Seagull"

Cillian Murphy's passion for the theatre extended beyond Ireland, leading him to perform on some of the world's most prestigious stages. In 2020, he starred in the National Theatre's production of Anton Chekhov's "The Seagull," directed by Ian Rickson.

His portrayal of Trigorin, a successful and self-absorbed writer, showcased his ability to delve into complex characters with psychological depth. Critics praised his performance for its sensitivity and emotional nuance, once again affirming Cillian's status as a formidable stage actor.

Challenges and Rewards of Live Performance

The theatre presented its own set of challenges and rewards for Cillian Murphy. Unlike film and television, where multiple takes and editing can enhance performance, the stage demanded unwavering commitment and precision from actors.

Live performances required Cillian to be fully present and immersed in the character's emotions, bringing the character to life in real time without the safety net of retakes. This level of vulnerability and immediacy forged a unique connection between Cillian and the audience, making each performance a truly unique and transformative experience.

The Impact of Theatre on Cillian's Craft

Cillian Murphy's work in the theatre had a profound impact on his approach to acting across all mediums. The discipline and rigor of live performances honed his skills as a performer, instilling in him a deep appreciation for the nuances of language, physicality, and emotional authenticity.

His experience in the theatre also allowed him to experiment with a wide range of roles, from classic plays to contemporary works, enabling him to continually push the boundaries of his craft. This diversity of roles enriched his understanding of the human psyche and contributed to his chameleon-like ability to inhabit a vast array of characters.

A Beacon for Aspiring Actors

Cillian Murphy's dedication to the theatre served as an inspiration to aspiring actors and artists. His willingness to return to the stage, despite achieving international fame, emphasized the profound impact of live performance on an actor's artistic growth and fulfillment.

As a respected figure in both Hollywood and the theatre world, Cillian became a beacon for young actors, encouraging them to embrace the stage as a vital platform for artistic expression. His commitment to maintaining a balance between film, television, and theatre demonstrated the significance of grounding oneself in the roots of one's craft, regardless of external recognition and success.

Conclusion

Chapter 6 delves into Cillian Murphy's enduring passion for the theatre and the profound impact of his live performances on his craft. Whether on Irish stages or prestigious international theatres, Cillian's dedication to the art of storytelling on stage enriched his journey as an actor and allowed him to continually challenge himself artistically.

His work in the theatre demonstrated the transformative power of live performance and reinforced his status as a versatile and deeply affecting actor. As he continued to embrace the stage throughout his career, Cillian Murphy remained committed to the timeless allure of live theatre, a medium that allowed him to connect with audiences on an intimate and profound level.

CHAPTER 7: MASTERING THE ART OF TRANSFORMATIO N

C illian Murphy's career has been marked by his remarkable ability to undergo physical and emotional transformations for his roles. Chapter 7 explores how Cillian's chameleon-like talent for embodying a diverse array of characters has solidified his reputation as an actor who is willing to push the boundaries of his craft and continually challenge himself.

Physical Transformations

One of the most striking aspects of Cillian Murphy's performances is his willingness to undergo significant physical transformations to fully inhabit his characters. From drastic changes in hairstyle and weight to alterations in posture and mannerisms, Cillian spares no effort in embodying the essence of his roles.

For his role as the transgender woman in "Breakfast on Pluto," Cillian donned feminine clothing, adopted a unique gait, and perfected the subtle nuances of femininity, creating a fully realized and authentic character. Similarly, in "Peaky Blinders," he transformed into the dapper and commanding Tommy Shelby, donning tailored suits, cropped hair, and adopting the Brummie accent to convincingly portray the charismatic gang leader.

Cillian's dedication to physical transformations not only adds authenticity to his performances but also demonstrates his commitment to fully immersing himself in each character's world, irrespective of the challenges involved.

The Power of Makeup and Prosthetics

In addition to his physical efforts, Cillian Murphy has also embraced the transformative power of makeup and prosthetics in his roles. The prosthetic

Scarecrow mask he wore in Christopher Nolan's "Batman Begins" concealed his face, allowing him to express the character's menace through voice and body language. This allowed him to focus on the psychology of the character and deliver a truly haunting performance.

Similarly, in "Peaky Blinders," Cillian's use of carefully crafted makeup and facial scars further brought Tommy Shelby to life, adding depth and complexity to the character's backstory and persona. These artistic choices showcase Cillian's willingness to use every available tool to enhance his performances and elevate his characters beyond the page.

Emotional Depth and Psychological Exploration

Beyond the physical aspects of transformation, Cillian Murphy's performances also delve deep into the emotional and psychological dimensions of his characters. His ability to convey a wide range of emotions with subtlety and nuance has been a hallmark of his work.

In "Red Eye," he portrayed a sinister villain, tapping into a menacing and cold-blooded persona that was chilling in its authenticity. In contrast, in "The Wind That Shakes the Barley," he captured the profound anguish and conflict of a young man torn between loyalty to family and the fight for independence. Cillian's emotional range and commitment to psychological exploration allow him to breathe life into complex and multi-dimensional characters.

Immersion in Preparation

Cillian Murphy's transformative performances are not the result of superficial mimicry but rather a result of thorough preparation and immersive research. He has spoken about the importance of understanding the context and historical background of his characters to bring them to life authentically.

For "The Wind That Shakes the Barley," Cillian studied the Irish War of Independence and the social and political climate of the time to better grasp the motivations and struggles of his character. His dedication to research allows him to infuse his performances with a depth of knowledge and understanding that elevates his portrayal beyond surface-level mimicry.

Pushing Boundaries in "Disco Pigs"

One of Cillian Murphy's earliest roles, "Disco Pigs," showcases his early mastery of transformation. As Pig, a volatile and disturbed teenager, Cillian's intense and raw portrayal allowed audiences to glimpse into the inner workings of an intricately troubled mind.

His performance in "Disco Pigs" was a revelation, earning him widespread acclaim and establishing him as an actor willing to tackle challenging and psychologically demanding roles. The experience of embodying such a complex character laid the foundation for his future transformations and served as a testament to his dedication to the craft.

Exploring Dark Realms in "Peacock"

In "Peacock," Cillian Murphy took on the formidable task of portraying dual characters – John Skillpa and Emma, his alter ego. This deeply psychological thriller explored themes of dissociative identity disorder and allowed Cillian to demonstrate his mastery of psychological complexity.

The film required Cillian to inhabit two distinct personalities, each with their own emotional and psychological intricacies. His ability to navigate the intricate dynamics between the two characters demonstrated his profound understanding of the human psyche and his commitment to exploring the darkest corners of the human mind.

Unconventional Roles: "The Dark Knight" and "Inception"

Cillian Murphy's collaboration with Christopher Nolan resulted in two iconic and unconventional roles. As the Scarecrow in "The Dark Knight," he portrayed a villain with a twisted fascination for inducing fear in others. His performance showcased a chilling and mesmerizing presence, transcending traditional villain roles.

In "Inception," Cillian took on the role of Robert Fischer, a seemingly innocent target with deep emotional complexities. His portrayal added layers of vulnerability and depth to the character, defying the typical stereotypes of antagonist roles.

Inspiring Future Generations

Cillian Murphy's transformative approach to acting has not only earned him critical acclaim but also inspired aspiring actors to challenge their boundaries. His dedication to fully immersing himself in his characters serves as a shining example of the commitment required to achieve authenticity in storytelling.

As an actor who continually seeks out diverse

and complex roles, Cillian encourages future generations of performers to embrace the art of transformation and explore the limitless potential of their craft.

Conclusion

Chapter 7 highlights Cillian Murphy's mastery of the art of transformation, both physically and emotionally. His willingness to undergo physical changes, immerse himself in research, and delve into the psyches of complex characters has set him apart as a transformative and extraordinary actor.

Cillian's ability to embody a vast range of characters has solidified his status as a versatile and enigmatic performer who continues to captivate audiences with each new role. His dedication to authenticity and psychological exploration has earned him acclaim and admiration from both peers and critics, leaving an indelible mark on the world of acting.

CHAPTER 8: COLLABORATION S AND RELATIONSHIPS

Cillian Murphy's journey in the entertainment industry has been defined not only by his extraordinary talent but also by the meaningful collaborations he has forged with fellow actors, directors, and creatives. Chapter 8 explores the significant relationships that have shaped Cillian's career, highlighting the transformative impact of these collaborations on his artistic growth and the enduring friendships he has cultivated along the way.

Enda Walsh: A Profound Partnership

One of the most significant and enduring collaborations in Cillian Murphy's career has been with Irish playwright Enda Walsh. Their partnership began with the acclaimed play "Disco Pigs," which marked a breakthrough moment for Cillian as an actor. Enda's raw and compelling writing combined with Cillian's intense portrayal of the troubled character Pig left an indelible impression on audiences and critics alike.

Their creative synergy continued with the play "Ballyturk" (2014), where Cillian once again showcased his versatility and emotional depth under Enda Walsh's direction. The power of their collaboration lies in their shared understanding of storytelling and their ability to push artistic boundaries, creating captivating and emotionally resonant performances.

Christopher Nolan: A Dynamic Duo

Cillian Murphy's collaboration with director Christopher Nolan has been one of the defining aspects of his career. Their partnership began with "Batman Begins" (2005), where Cillian played the sinister Scarecrow. Nolan's unique vision for the Batman trilogy allowed Cillian to bring complexity and depth to the character, elevating the role beyond typical villain portrayals.

Their collaboration continued with "The Dark Knight" (2008) and "Inception" (2010), where Cillian portrayed Robert Fischer, adding emotional depth to the character. Nolan's trust in Cillian's talent and his willingness to challenge the actor with unconventional roles has solidified their partnership as one of the most fruitful in contemporary cinema.

Danny Boyle: A Directorial Connection

Cillian Murphy's connection with director Danny Boyle spans multiple projects, including "28 Days Later" (2002) and "Sunshine" (2007). Boyle's unique directorial style and penchant for unconventional storytelling provided the perfect platform for Cillian to showcase his versatility.

In "28 Days Later," Cillian delivered a memorable performance as Jim, a survivor in a post-apocalyptic world. The film's critical and commercial success catapulted Cillian to international fame. "Sunshine" further showcased Cillian's ability to anchor a film with emotional depth and complexity.

Their collaborations demonstrate a mutual understanding of storytelling and a shared vision for bringing unconventional narratives to life.

Peaky Blinders: A Family on and Off Screen

Cillian Murphy's portrayal of Tommy Shelby in the television series "Peaky Blinders" has not only become iconic but has also forged lasting friendships among the cast and crew. The camaraderie and chemistry among the cast members, including Helen McCrory, Paul Anderson, and Tom Hardy, have contributed to the show's immense popularity.

Behind the scenes, the cast and crew have spoken about the close-knit family atmosphere on set, which has allowed for a strong sense of collaboration and creativity. The success of "Peaky Blinders" has further solidified Cillian's status as a prominent television actor and has led to many memorable interactions with fans worldwide.

The National Theatre: A Reunion with Talent

Cillian Murphy's collaboration with the National Theatre in productions such as "The Seagull" (2020) allowed him to work with esteemed directors and fellow actors in the theatre world. His performances on such prestigious stages demonstrated his adaptability as an actor and his commitment to the art of live theatre.

Working with the National Theatre allowed Cillian to engage with classic works and collaborate with renowned theatre professionals, adding to the depth and breadth of his artistic experiences.

John Crowley: An Ongoing Working Relationship

Director John Crowley has also played a significant role in Cillian Murphy's career. Their collaboration began with "Intermission" (2003), a darkly comedic Irish film, where Cillian portrayed a character embroiled in a series of interconnected stories. Their partnership continued with "Boy A" (2007), a drama that showcased Cillian's ability to convey profound emotional depth.

Their ongoing working relationship is a testament to the mutual respect and understanding between actor and director, allowing for a seamless creative process and compelling on-screen performances.

Inspiring and Supporting Peers

Throughout his career, Cillian Murphy has also been an advocate for fellow actors and creatives. He has consistently praised the talent and dedication of his co-stars, and his collaborative spirit has fostered a positive and supportive atmosphere on set.

Cillian's ability to create a sense of camaraderie and mutual respect among his peers has contributed to the success and harmony of various productions.

The Impact of Collaboration on Cillian's Artistry

The meaningful collaborations in Cillian Murphy's career have had a profound impact on his artistry as an actor. Working with visionary directors and fellow actors has allowed him to continually push the boundaries of his craft, explore diverse characters, and grow as an artist.

These collaborations have provided him with a rich and varied canvas upon which to hone his skills, delivering performances that are both emotionally authentic and visually compelling.

Conclusion

Chapter 8 explores the transformative power of collaborations and relationships in Cillian Murphy's career. His partnerships with esteemed playwrights, directors, and fellow actors have allowed him to evolve as an artist, continually pushing the boundaries of his craft and delivering captivating performances.

From his enduring connection with Enda Walsh to his dynamic collaborations with Christopher Nolan and Danny Boyle, these creative partnerships have not only shaped Cillian's career but have also enriched the world of cinema and theatre.

As Cillian Murphy continues to forge new collaborations and nurture existing relationships, his artistic journey remains marked by a commitment to storytelling, a willingness to embrace challenges, and an enduring passion for the craft of acting.

CHAPTER 9: BALANCING FAME AND PRIVACY

As Cillian Murphy's career reached new heights, the balancing act between fame and privacy became an intricate challenge. Chapter 9 delves into the complexities of navigating the public eye while safeguarding his personal life, exploring how Cillian has managed to strike a delicate balance between his rising celebrity status and his desire for a private existence.

The Rise to International Fame

Cillian Murphy's breakthrough performances in critically acclaimed films such as "28 Days Later," "Batman Begins," and "Inception" catapulted him to international stardom. As his fame grew, so did public interest in his personal life. Red carpet events, interviews, and media appearances became a regular part of his professional life.

The heightened attention presented both opportunities and challenges for Cillian, who valued his privacy but also recognized the importance of connecting with fans and promoting his work.

The Private Persona

Cillian Murphy's private nature has been evident throughout his career. He has often expressed discomfort with the spotlight and is known for keeping his personal life out of the tabloids. Despite his celebrity status, he remains guarded about his family, relationships, and personal experiences.

Instead of courting the media, Cillian has preferred to let his work speak for itself, allowing his performances and artistic choices to be the primary focus of public attention.

The Impact on Family and Loved Ones

As public interest in Cillian's life increased, so did the scrutiny faced by his family and loved ones. Paparazzi and media attention can be invasive and disruptive, affecting the lives of those closest to the actor. Cillian's desire to shield his loved ones from the public eye is a testament to his commitment to protecting their privacy and well-being.

Maintaining a healthy and grounded personal life away from the spotlight has been crucial for Cillian, as it allows him to recharge and preserve his emotional and creative energy.

Navigating Social Media

In an era of digital communication and social media, celebrities often face additional challenges in managing their public personas. While some actors embrace social media as a platform to connect with fans, Cillian Murphy has chosen to keep his distance from these platforms.

His absence from social media allows him greater control over his public image and privacy. It also reinforces the idea that his work as an actor speaks loudest, rather than the curated narratives that social media can perpetuate.

Interviews and Public Appearances

Cillian Murphy approaches interviews and public appearances with a focus on his work and the projects he is involved in. While he may share insights into his characters and creative process, he tends to keep personal details to a minimum.

His interviews are marked by a thoughtful and introspective approach, reflecting his deep commitment to the art of acting. By keeping the focus on his craft, Cillian can maintain boundaries while still engaging with the media and his audience.

Fostering Respectful Boundaries

Cillian Murphy's ability to balance fame and privacy stems from his conscious efforts to set respectful boundaries with the media and the public. While he recognizes the interest and support of his fans, he remains committed to safeguarding his personal life.

He has often spoken about the importance of drawing a line between his public and private selves, ensuring that the spotlight remains on his work as an actor rather than on his personal life.

Retreat to Ireland

A significant aspect of maintaining privacy for Cillian has been his retreat to Ireland, where he spends a considerable amount of time with his family. Ireland holds a special place in his heart, and it allows him a respite from the hectic pace of the entertainment industry.

The serene and close-knit community in Ireland has provided a refuge for Cillian, allowing him to strike a balance between his public and private life while staying connected to his roots.

Preserving Normalcy

Despite his international fame, Cillian Murphy strives to maintain a sense of normalcy in his life. He has been spotted engaging in everyday activities such as walking his dogs or cycling around town, emphasizing that he is just an ordinary person who happens to have an extraordinary career.

Preserving a semblance of normalcy allows Cillian to ground himself and maintain perspective amidst the whirlwind of fame and attention.

The Impact on Fans and Admirers

Cillian Murphy's approach to balancing fame and privacy has garnered admiration and respect from his fans and admirers. While some celebrities may fully embrace the public eye, Cillian's understated and private demeanor resonates with many who appreciate his commitment to his craft and his refusal to let fame overshadow his artistic integrity.

His decision to focus on his work rather than cultivating a celebrity persona has endeared him to audiences who appreciate authenticity and artistry in the world of entertainment.

Conclusion

Chapter 9 explores the intricacies of Cillian Murphy's journey in balancing fame and privacy. As his career reached new heights, he faced the challenges of navigating the public eye while protecting his personal life and loved ones from excessive scrutiny.

Cillian's commitment to maintaining a private persona, shielding his family from media attention, and preserving a sense of normalcy has allowed him to find harmony amid fame. His focus on his work as an actor, rather than cultivating a celebrity persona, has endeared him to audiences and admirers who value his authenticity and dedication to the art of storytelling.

As he continues to evolve as an actor, Cillian Murphy's ability to strike a delicate balance between fame and privacy remains a testament to his strength of character and the genuine passion he holds for his craft.

CHAPTER 10: PERSONAL LIFE

B ehind the fame and accolades, Cillian Murphy maintains a private and grounded personal life. This chapter delves into the actor's relationships, family, hobbies, and the values that shape his off-screen existence. While Cillian's work as an actor has garnered international recognition, his personal life reflects a commitment to authenticity, connection, and a profound appreciation for the simple joys of living.

Family and Relationships

Cillian Murphy places great value on his family and relationships, cherishing his role as a husband and father. In 2004, he married his long-time girlfriend, Yvonne McGuinness, an accomplished visual artist, and director. The couple's relationship is characterized by its privacy and mutual support.

Together, they have two sons, Malachy and Aran, with whom Cillian shares a loving and nurturing bond. Despite his fame, Cillian has managed to shield his family from the public eye, allowing them to maintain a sense of normalcy away from the spotlight.

Life in Ireland

Born and raised in Ireland, Cillian Murphy's connection to his homeland remains a cornerstone of his personal life. He has often spoken about his deep love for Ireland, its rich cultural heritage, and the sense of community that it offers.

Cillian's affinity for Ireland extends beyond his career, and he spends considerable time in the country, particularly in County Cork, where he grew up. Embracing a down-to-earth lifestyle, he enjoys cycling, walking his dogs, and engaging in everyday activities that emphasize his commitment to preserving a sense of normalcy.

Appreciation for Privacy

Cillian Murphy's appreciation for privacy extends beyond his family life. He has consistently expressed his desire to keep his personal life out of the public eye and maintains a selective approach to media engagement.

While Cillian acknowledges the support of his fans and the interest in his work, he remains committed to maintaining respectful boundaries and protecting his personal space. This guarded approach to fame has earned him admiration from both fans and fellow celebrities who value his dedication to preserving a sense of privacy.

Engagement with Fans

Despite his privacy preference, Cillian Murphy remains appreciative of his fans and their support. He has participated in fan events, Q&A sessions, and charity initiatives, which allow him to engage with admirers on his terms.

His interactions with fans are characterized by humility and genuine gratitude, underscoring his commitment to forging authentic connections with those who appreciate his work as an actor.

A Love for Music

Outside of his acting career, Cillian Murphy has a passion for music. He is an accomplished musician, proficient in playing the guitar and singing. His love for music has led him to explore various musical projects, including a collaboration with Irish musician and composer Neil Hannon.

Music serves as a creative outlet and a source of joy for Cillian, complementing his dedication to the arts and providing an opportunity to express his artistic sensibilities beyond the realm of acting.

Environmental Advocacy

Cillian Murphy's commitment to environmental causes is another significant aspect of his personal life. He has been an advocate for sustainable living and has been involved in initiatives that promote environmental conservation and awareness.

His dedication to environmental advocacy aligns with his appreciation for nature and the Irish countryside, where he finds solace and inspiration away from the hustle and bustle of the entertainment industry.

Humble and Grounded Demeanor

Despite his immense success, Cillian Murphy maintains a humble and grounded demeanor. He is known for his polite and respectful interactions with colleagues, fans, and the media. Colleagues and co-stars often praise his professionalism, work ethic, and ability to foster a positive and collaborative atmosphere on set.

Cillian's humility and down-to-earth attitude have endeared him to those who work with him, reinforcing his reputation as an actor who values his craft and remains committed to genuine human connections.

Balance between Personal and Professional Life

Throughout his career, Cillian Murphy has demonstrated a keen ability to strike a balance between his personal and professional life. Despite his international fame, he remains committed to his family and the values that ground him as an individual.

The support of his family and their shared appreciation for privacy has allowed Cillian to navigate the demands of fame without losing sight of his identity beyond his career as an actor.

Conclusion

Chapter 10 delves into Cillian Murphy's personal life, revealing a man deeply committed to his family,

Ireland, and the values that shape his off-screen existence. Despite achieving international fame, he remains grounded and appreciative of the privacy that allows him to maintain a sense of normalcy in his daily life.

His humility, engagement with fans on his terms, love for music, and dedication to environmental advocacy demonstrate a multifaceted individual with a profound appreciation for the simple joys of living. Balancing fame and private personal life, Cillian Murphy's journey as an actor and an individual reflects authenticity, genuine connections, and a commitment to his craft and values beyond the spotlight.

CHAPTER 11: LEGACY AND INFLUENCE

As Cillian Murphy's career continues to thrive, his legacy as an actor and his influence on the world of entertainment become increasingly evident. Chapter 11 explores the lasting impact of Cillian's work, how he has inspired aspiring actors and the contributions he has made to the film and theatre industries.

A Diverse and Impressive Body of Work

Cillian Murphy's legacy is built on a diverse and impressive body of work that spans film, television, and theatre. His willingness to take on challenging and unconventional roles has earned him critical acclaim and respect from both peers and critics.

From his breakthrough role in "Disco Pigs" to his memorable performances in "28 Days Later," "The Wind That Shakes the Barley," and "Peaky Blinders," Cillian has continuously showcased his versatility, emotional depth, and commitment to authenticity. His body of work stands as a testament to his dedication to the craft of acting and the power of storytelling.

Championing Authenticity in Acting

Throughout his career, Cillian Murphy has championed authenticity in acting, emphasizing the importance of emotional depth, psychological exploration, and immersive preparation. His transformative performances, both physically and emotionally, have set a standard for aspiring actors seeking to embody complex and multi-dimensional characters.

Cillian's dedication to authenticity has inspired a new generation of performers to approach their craft with honesty, vulnerability, and a commitment to delving into the depths of the characters they portray.

Balancing Film, Television, and Theatre

Cillian Murphy's ability to balance his work in film, television, and theatre has broadened his impact on the entertainment industry. By excelling in multiple mediums, he has showcased the power of storytelling across different platforms and highlighted the unique strengths of each form of art.

His willingness to return to the theatre despite international fame has emphasized the importance of grounding oneself in the roots of acting and embracing the intimate connection with live audiences. Cillian's versatility as an actor has made him a respected figure in both Hollywood and the theatre world, inspiring others to explore and embrace various creative opportunities.

Elevating Supporting Roles

Cillian Murphy's legacy also includes his exceptional ability to elevate supporting roles, making them just as memorable and significant as leading characters. His portrayals of supporting characters are marked by nuance, complexity, and a profound impact on the overall narrative.

Whether it is the enigmatic Scarecrow in "Batman Begins" or the charming Robert Fischer in "Inception," Cillian's commitment to fully embodying supporting roles has demonstrated the profound influence a talented actor can have on a film's storytelling, beyond the confines of the lead character.

A Versatile Chameleon

Cillian Murphy's chameleon-like talent for transformation has left a lasting impression on the industry. His ability to immerse himself physically and emotionally in a vast array of characters has inspired fellow actors to push the boundaries of their craft and embrace the transformative power of performance.

His portrayal of characters with depth and authenticity has proven that an actor's ability to fully inhabit roles can create an indelible impact on audiences and elevate the storytelling experience.

A Source of Inspiration for Peers

Cillian Murphy's work ethic, dedication to the art of acting, and grounded persona have made him a source of inspiration for his peers. Fellow actors and directors have spoken highly of his professionalism, commitment to collaboration, and the supportive atmosphere he fosters on set.

His ability to maintain a private personal life despite fame has earned him admiration from colleagues, who value his focus on authentic connections and genuine interactions, both on and off-screen.

Contributing to Irish Cinema

As an Irish actor with a global presence, Cillian Murphy has contributed significantly to the visibility and recognition of Irish cinema on the international stage. His involvement in both Irish and international productions has served to bridge the gap between the two worlds and highlight the talent and creativity of Irish filmmakers and actors.

His continued dedication to working in Ireland and supporting the country's film industry has made him an ambassador for Irish cinema and a role model for aspiring Irish actors.

Cultural Impact and Enduring Relevance

Cillian Murphy's cultural impact and enduring relevance can be seen in the continued popularity of his work and the lasting influence he has on the entertainment industry. His performances are celebrated and studied by actors and directors, and his characters have become iconic in the world of cinema and television.

Beyond his artistic achievements, Cillian's authenticity, and commitment to staying true to himself have resonated with audiences and contributed to his continued relevance and appeal as an actor.

A Legacy of Authenticity and Dedication

In conclusion, Chapter 11 explores Cillian Murphy's legacy and influence on the world of entertainment. His commitment to authenticity, dedication to his craft, and ability to embrace diverse roles have left a profound impact on the industry and inspired aspiring actors to approach their work with integrity and passion.

As Cillian Murphy continues to evolve as an actor and a person, his legacy as a versatile and transformative performer will undoubtedly endure, leaving an indelible mark on the world of film, television, and theatre for generations to come.

CHAPTER 12:
BEYOND ACTING:
VENTURES
AND FUTURE
ENDEAVORS

Cillian Murphy's artistic journey extends beyond acting, as he has ventured into various creative pursuits and expressed a desire to explore new challenges in the future. Chapter 12 delves into Cillian's diverse interests, including his foray into directing, music, and potential future endeavors, as he continues to leave his mark on the world of entertainment in multifaceted ways.

Exploring Directing

In addition to his illustrious acting career, Cillian Murphy has expressed a keen interest in exploring the world of directing. While he has yet to direct a feature film, he took on the directorial role for the critically acclaimed short film "The Party" (2017).

"The Party" showcased Cillian's storytelling prowess from behind the camera, demonstrating his ability to craft a compelling narrative and draw authentic performances from actors. His venture into directing earned him praise from peers and critics alike, fueling anticipation for potential future projects as a director.

Cillian's experience as an actor allows him a unique perspective when directing, and his dedication to authenticity and emotional depth can undoubtedly translate to his work behind the camera. As he continues to expand his horizons, the prospect of Cillian Murphy's further explorations as a director remains an exciting and promising aspect of his future endeavors.

A Passion for Music

Music has been an integral part of Cillian Murphy's

life, and his passion for the art form extends beyond playing the guitar and singing. He has often collaborated with musicians and composers, further immersing himself in the world of music.

One of his notable collaborations includes working with Irish musician and composer Neil Hannon, with whom he performed and recorded music. His love for music has provided him with an avenue for creative expression beyond acting, allowing him to connect with audiences through yet another artistic medium.

Continued Commitment to Theatre

Cillian Murphy's dedication to the theatre remains unwavering, despite his international fame in film and television. Throughout his career, he has returned to the stage to engage with live audiences and embrace the intimacy and immediacy of theatrical performances.

His involvement with esteemed theatre companies and directors, such as the National Theatre and Enda Walsh, reflects his commitment to preserving the rich tradition of live theatre and pushing its boundaries as an art form.

Cillian's profound connection to the theatre world

reinforces his status as an actor devoted to the craft and underscores the significance of his roots in acting.

Philanthropic Efforts

Beyond his creative pursuits, Cillian Murphy has been involved in philanthropic endeavors, supporting charitable causes and initiatives close to his heart. While he tends to keep these efforts private, his commitment to environmental advocacy has been evident in his public statements and actions.

As a vocal advocate for sustainable living and environmental conservation, Cillian's influence extends beyond the entertainment industry and serves as an example of using fame and influence for positive change.

The Allure of Complex Characters

Throughout his career, Cillian Murphy has been drawn to portraying complex and psychologically intriguing characters. He has expressed a preference for roles that challenge him as an actor and allow him to explore the depths of human emotions.

His affinity for multi-dimensional characters has

become a hallmark of his work and a driving force behind his artistic choices. As he looks towards future projects, it is evident that Cillian will continue to seek out roles that challenge and inspire him, and that showcase his commitment to authenticity and storytelling.

Future Collaborations and Artistic Challenges

As Cillian Murphy's career progresses, he remains open to future collaborations and artistic challenges. His desire to continually explore and grow as an actor and artist reflects his dedication to the craft and his willingness to push the boundaries of his abilities.

Cillian's collaborative spirit and respect for his peers have earned him admiration from fellow actors and directors, further solidifying his position as a respected figure in the entertainment industry.

The Power of Legacy

Cillian Murphy's legacy is already well-established, with his impact on the world of entertainment evident through his diverse body of work and influence on aspiring actors. As he continues to explore new creative avenues, his legacy will undoubtedly grow, leaving a lasting imprint on the industry and inspiring future generations of performers.

His commitment to authenticity, dedication to his craft, and engagement with meaningful storytelling serve as a reminder of the transformative power of art and the profound impact actors can have on the lives of audiences.

Conclusion

Chapter 12 examines Cillian Murphy's ventures beyond acting, including his interest in directing, passion for music, continued commitment to theatre, and philanthropic efforts. As he explores new challenges and artistic endeavors, Cillian's dedication to authenticity, storytelling, and growth as an artist remains central to his journey.

His legacy as an actor and an individual continues to evolve, leaving an indelible mark on the world of entertainment and inspiring others to embrace their creativity and pursue their passions with unwavering dedication.

As Cillian Murphy's artistic journey unfolds, his influence will extend far beyond the screen and the stage, shaping the future of the entertainment industry and inspiring aspiring artists to explore the limitless potential of their craft.

APPENDIX

Filmography and Theatreography

Filmography:

1. "Sunburn" (1999) - Davin McDerby

2. "The Trench" (1999) - Rag Rookwood

3. "Disco Pigs" (2001) - Pig

4. "How Harry Became a Tree" (2001) - Gus

5. "On the Edge" (2001) - Jonathan Breech

6. "28 Days Later" (2002) - Jim

7. "Cold Mountain" (2003) - Bardolph

8. "Girl with a Pearl Earring" (2003) - Pieter

9. "Intermission" (2003) - John

10. "The Girl in the Café" (2005) - Lawrence

11. "Red Eye" (2005) - Jackson Rippner

12. "Batman Begins" (2005) - Dr. Jonathan Crane / Scarecrow

13. "Breakfast on Pluto" (2005) - Patrick "Kitten" Braden

14. "The Wind That Shakes the Barley" (2006) - Damien O'Donovan

15. "The Dark Knight" (2008) - Dr. Jonathan Crane / Scarecrow (cameo)

16. "Perrier's Bounty" (2009) - Michael McCrea

17. "Inception" (2010) - Robert Fischer

18. "Tron: Legacy" (2010) - Edward Dillinger Jr. (cameo)

19. "Peacock" (2010) - John Skillpa / Emma Skillpa

20. "In Time" (2011) - Timekeeper Raymond Leon

21. "Red Lights" (2012) - Tom Buckley

22. "Broken" (2012) - Mike Kiernan

23. "Transcendence" (2014) - Agent Donald Buchanan

24. "Aloft" (2014) - Ivan

25. "In the Heart of the Sea" (2015) - Matthew Joy

26. "Free Fire" (2016) - Chris

27. "Dunkirk" (2017) - Shivering Soldier

28. "The Party" (2017) - Director (short film)

29. "Anna" (2019) - Lenny Miller

30. "A Quiet Place Part II" (2020) - Emmett

Television:

1. "The Way We Live Now" (2001) - Paul Montague

2. "The Clinic" (2003) - Dr. Mike

3. "The Silent City" (2006) - Narrator (documentary)

4. "Broken" (2017) - Father Michael Kerrigan

5. "Peaky Blinders" (2013-2022) - Thomas "Tommy" Shelby

Theatreography:

1. "Disco Pigs" (1996) - Pig

2. "Juno and the Paycock" (1998) - Johnny Boyle

3. "Much Ado About Nothing" (1999) - Benedick

4. "The Playboy of the Western World" (2006) - Christy Mahon

5. "The Seagull" (2012) - Konstantin Treplyov

6. "Ballyturk" (2014) - 1

7. "Grief is the Thing with Feathers" (2018) - Dad

INFO EDGE

You are a contributor to the Reading Revolution which Info Edge is bringing by digitalising and economising the book industry. Founded in 2021, Info Edge Publications is working towards providing quality content and making books affordable for all. We believe that knowledge is everyone's birthright and one shall get it. Info Edge is selling in 13 countries across the globe with a global vision. Please do follow us on -

*Instagram - **@theinfoedgepub***
*Twitter - **@theinfoedgepub***

You can also leave us feedback by mail at -

infoedgecorp@gmail.com

Printed in Great Britain
by Amazon